Quickbooks

The ultimate guide to Quickbooks, including accounting basics and bookkeeping!

Table of Contents

Introduction 1

Chapter 1: Accounting vs. Bookkeeping 2

Chapter 2: The Need for Accounting Software 4

Chapter 3: Accounting Software vs. Spreadsheets 7

Chapter 4: What is Quickbooks? 10

Chapter 5: How Businesses Use Quickbooks 11

Chapter 6: The Different Versions of Quickbooks 15

Chapter 7: The Various Features of Quickbooks 29

Chapter 8: How to Navigate Quickbooks 34

Chapter 9: How to Create Financial Reports Using Quickbooks 36

Chapter 10: How to Perform Basic Accounting Functions in Quickbooks 40

Chapter 11: Troubleshooting 43

Chapter 12: Quickbooks Shortcuts 47

Chapter 13: Frequently Asked Questions 51

Conclusion 63

Introduction

Thank you for taking the time to pick up this book about Quickbooks!

This book aims to serve as a guide to using Quickbooks for all of your accounting needs! Whether you have any accounting experience or not, Quickbooks makes managing your businesses' finances simple.

In the following chapters, we cover the different versions of Quickbooks that are available, the benefits and features of each, and which might be the best for your particular needs.

Later, we cover how to perform a variety of functions within the Quickbooks program, including how to manage and view the taxes you may owe, how to create a variety of reports, and how to navigate the Quickbooks platform. Also included is a handy list of Quickbooks shortcuts, and a comprehensive FAQ list that will help to make you a pro Quickbooks user in no time!

At the completion of this book you will have a good understanding of Quickbooks, and be ready to use it in your own business!

Once again, thanks for choosing this book, I hope you find it to be helpful!

Chapter 1: Accounting vs. Bookkeeping

Considering accounting and bookkeeping to be the same practice is a very common misconception that people make. Although both are essential in business, there are several distinctions that differentiate the two practices.

With bookkeeping, you're talking about the recordkeeping process applied to various financial transactions. It's more basic in approach, and serves the purpose of helping business owners keep track of their daily income and expenses.

Accounting, on the other hand, involves a more comprehensive assessment of financial transactions. Here, professionals don't only record data, but classify, analyze, interpret, report, and summarize them as well, with the intention of determining how a business is doing — where it's achieving expectations and where it's falling short of projections.

Bookkeepers record transactions chronologically, daily. Depending on the company or software they're working with, they may also be tasked to be in charge of summarizing financial data for reports.

Meanwhile, accountants work with the same data and reports, but strictly abide by accounting principles and standards. Not only do they assess the condition of the business, but they also provide insights that will help business owners make informed decisions with regard to their operations.

Why They Seem Similar

To a layman, both may seem like the same profession. This is because bookkeeping and accounting deal with numbers, simply put. Both require professionals to have at least a basic grasp of accounting principles and practices.

In some cases — especially with smaller companies — bookkeepers often act as in-house accountants as well. Even without the same extent of knowledge, they can work on accounting-specific tasks, especially if they have the software to do so — the kind which automates almost everything for them.

How Accounting and Bookkeeping are Different

Bookkeepers only need to have a basic grasp of accounting, while accountants must have a bachelor's degree and certification in order to practice it. Accountants can manage all components of the accounting process and often oversee the bookkeepers' work to ensure that everything is accurate. Accountants are also the ones who provide the initial assessment of a company's financial health, explaining the situation to owners through a series of reports.

Chapter 2: The Need for Accounting Software

Accounting software is designed not only to help people manage income and expense transactions. It usually consists of a series of programs that vary in scope, some of which are designed to manage simple bookkeeping tasks, while others are meant to help with more complicated financial computations.

When accounting software is utilized, companies are better able to control their daily operations — and with this improved efficiency comes reduced costs (in terms of manpower hours), not to mention avoided mistakes (in the recording and reporting processes).

There are different reasons why entrepreneurs and businesses should consider using accounting software, and here are some of them:

1. Cost-Effectiveness

With enhanced efficiency comes the cost-effective benefit of utilizing accounting software. Although there's an investment (read: expense) that comes with purchasing and applying the program, users can experience returns rather quickly.

With almost everything automated by the system, each member of the accounting team will have more time to spare, thus giving them the chance to use these official hours to attend to their other professional responsibilities. Manpower can be allotted more effectively, thereby reducing overhead costs while enhancing productivity at the same time.

2. Speed and Efficiency

When there's an accounting program in use, businesses can process transactions quickly. As they say, time saved is money saved. Let's face it; Computers can process complex computations faster than the human brain does, so there really is great value in automation, especially for larger-scale businesses that have to deal with sizeable transaction lists.

You can program your software to manage everything, from recording and computing sales taxes, to monitoring payables and receivables, and processing payroll.

3. Accuracy in Calculation

You want to minimize human error when dealing with numbers, as these errors can be costly. With manual accounting methods comes the need for manual mathematical calculations. And one incorrect computation or data interpretation can lead to plenty of issues down the line. Fortunately, this is something that accounting software can help you with.

But this doesn't mean that the software will completely eliminate the problem, since there remains to be a human element in place. Nevertheless, you're assured of more accurate records moving forward as most of the number crunching is done through the system.

4. Easier Tax Filing

Every business is mandated by the government to file taxes every fiscal year; and doing so can be rather troublesome, not to mention time-consuming. With accounting software, you can easily automate tax calculations. This means that you only have to make a few clicks and the system will generate your tax returns right then and there.

5. Quicker Reports Generation

Apart from making the encoding, recording, and computing elements of the accounting process simpler, accounting software can make generating reports easier, too. If any member of the team needs, say, a cash flow report in an hour, it will only take a few clicks on the system for the report to be generated in a print-ready fashion. Most accounting software comes with different templates that allow for a wide variety of these reports to be created in a jiffy.

Chapter 3: Accounting Software vs. Spreadsheets

Most of the time, small business owners would rather go for something basic than spend on things like software. But the thing is, unless they are well aware of the financial condition of their business, foregoing reliable software could be a nail in their coffin. These days, entrepreneurs are heavily advised to use accounting programs and move away from spreadsheets.

Spreadsheets may look simple enough, and the best part is that they're free (especially if your computer is equipped with an office suite). But accounting via spreadsheets is not the smartest move you can make. One of the biggest issues accountants have with businesses that use spreadsheets is that they attempt to track expenses with it, and do so incorrectly. It's not that spreadsheets are completely bad, but they do have a purpose other than being used for monitoring transactions.

Why Choose Quickbooks Over Spreadsheets?

Quickbooks, or any accounting software for that matter, trumps spreadsheets in so many ways. Here are some of the reasons why you should definitely consider investing in an accounting program for your business:

1. Quickbooks has been developed by people who don't just understand the automation process, but accounting in its entirety as well. The thing about spreadsheets is that you have to devise your own plan, process, or strategy. In most occasions, especially if you aren't experienced in the field, this will not only be troublesome, but the results may not be optimal for your needs.

2. Quickbooks has the capacity to generate quality financial reports in a matter of minutes. Given its design, it can create everything from a profit and loss statement to a

balance sheet; depending on what you need. If you're using spreadsheets, you have to figure out how these are done. Again, the process can be problematic, not to mention time-consuming. Accuracy is another issue you might encounter with the latter.

3. With spreadsheets, formulas depend on the user. In this case, you might end up making formulaic errors and fail to notice them until it's too late. When it comes to business reports, being even a few cents off can make a huge difference in the outcome of your records. Quickbooks is programmed to deal with mathematical calculations so you can rest assured that you'll get accurate reports each and every time.

4. Another benefit of Quickbooks is that it provides users with electronic records of past and present transactions and reports. In the field of accounting, this kind of audit trail is highly valuable. With spreadsheets, you can manually print and file them or store them in an external drive or the cloud. And when the time comes for you to make updates, expect headaches.

5. Quickbooks allows you to send electronic invoices to your clients. Apart from creating a transaction record on a spreadsheet, you'll have to create separate files for invoices, payment orders, and other requests.

6. With spreadsheets, even something as simple as ownership of the master sheet can pose problems. With multiple individuals accessing the program, how will you know which version is the most recently updated one? It can be quite a hassle to manage something like this, while with Quickbooks, everything is updated on the system so you'll always be accessing the most recent version of your

records — even if the program's been accessed through different devices.

7. Quickbooks allows you to work on different devices, be it a phone, tablet, laptop, or desktop computer. With a spreadsheet, chances are that you'll be stuck on a computer.

8. If you don't have an in-house accountant, you can easily share access to your files or have an outsourcer work on your Quickbooks account. Good luck achieving the same thing with spreadsheets.

9. And of course, the accountant will be working with standard accounting systems and templates when on Quickbooks. With a spreadsheet, he or she will still have to figure out the accounting system you've set in place.

Chapter 4: What is Quickbooks?

Quickbooks was created by a company called Intuit, which was founded by Tom Proulx and Scott Cook in the USA in 1983. Intuit created a financial management platform called Quicken, but it was meant for large corporations. In order to capture the market of small-to medium-sized businesses, they came up with Quickbooks.

The first release was rather basic. It really didn't offer double-entry accounting components. But as time progressed, and with more users patronizing the software, the company was able to improve Quickbooks to offer a multitude of accounting functionalities that conform to traditional accounting standards.

There are different types of software available for managing various accounting processes, and Quickbooks is a comprehensive program that falls into this category. This program can be used to monitor sales and expenses, and create reports for businesses of different scales. Depending on the version you choose to purchase, some also provide the tools that you'll need to create and send invoices, pay bills, file taxes, and the like.

Quickbooks is the kind of program that can service entrepreneurs, small business owners, and mid-scale organizations. In this case, you have to choose the right version of Quickbooks given your business needs. It's good to know that there even is a version that caters to industry-specific businesses. And users need not shell out money immediately. This program has a try-before-you-buy option, so you can test it out for 30 days before deciding whether or not to buy or subscribe.

Chapter 5: How Businesses Use Quickbooks

Quickbooks is the type of accounting software that's ideal for small-to-medium-sized businesses. Usually, the program is used by business owners to manage their daily transactions, from invoices to bills. It enables them to have better control over their receivables, payables, and other components that are linked to their cash flow.

There are some versions that even offer support for year-end financial reporting, with tax computations included. Reports generation is another functionality that Quickbooks users depend on, as the system can generate a series of reports with just a few clicks.

The beauty of Quickbooks is that it can be used by in-house bookkeepers or accountants, and can also be shared should the company decide to work with outsourced personnel. It is also possible for businesses to have people work on the system simultaneously and across different devices.

Here are some of the ways Quickbooks is being used daily by its patrons:

1. Income Monitoring

Users have the capacity to track their sales and income streams using Quickbooks because it allows them to create track-able invoices with ease. These invoices can be categorized by the customer for easier navigation and better control. Because of this, users can easily check receivable balances via the Accounts Receivable Aging Report, which presents not only the details of current invoices, but also the status of those that are past due (how much the totals are, and for how long they've been due).

2. Expense Tracking

Just like how users can rely on Quickbooks to help them monitor the money that's coming into the business, it can also be of assistance when it comes to keeping track of expenses and other relevant billings. In this case, users can link their bank accounts and credit card numbers to the platform, allowing for easy data downloading and expense categorization, plus monitoring. Should there be an occasion when a user finds the need to track an issued check, for example, this can immediately be recorded in the system.

When it comes to paying bills, users have access to a feature that makes this possible. Businesses can rest assured that paying bills on time will no longer be problematic. Not only will they receive notifications or reminders, but they can also address the need digitally. Because the system is able to generate an Accounts Payable Report, you get all the necessary details in a matter of minutes.

3. Inventory Monitoring

If you just so happen to have inventories as part of your daily ops, you'll be happy to know that inventory tracking is yet another feature that Quickbooks is equipped with. With it, you can track quantities, unit costs, on-hand totals (products and amounts), and so on. Quickbooks will do the work for you — updating the lists with every transaction you enter into the system. If you need it, you can also generate inventory reports whenever, and from wherever. You might be thinking that the same can be done on a spreadsheet. Well, it can, but the task will be rather time-consuming.

4. Payroll Generation

No matter how small the business is, payroll is one thing business owners can't take lightly. As much as possible, you shouldn't do it manually as doing so will open doors for costly mistakes, penalties, or worse; unhappy workers. With

Quickbooks, users gain access to a payroll feature which computes salaries as often as necessary. And by using it to generate payroll, your financial statements will always be updated to include this expense. Provided that your Quickbooks version is constantly updated, all of the latest tax tables will already be integrated into the system. Now that's one less thing for you to worry about.

With Quickbooks, you can enjoy these added benefits in line with payroll:

- Direct or e-pay employees from the system
- Automatic tax computations
- Automatic generation of tax reports

5. Reports Generation

Considering how the program helps you manage cash flows, it becomes a whole lot easier to generate reports and insights whenever the business needs them. A number of different reports can be generated using Quickbooks, and it only takes a few clicks to get the generation phase started. Based on the data you input into the system, the reports are automatically updated as well. When you need to present financials to the board, partners, or potential investors, being able to create them with ease and a heightened sense of accuracy matters.

Some of the reports that can be generated here include:

- *Balance Sheet*
  When it comes to the balance sheet, you'll see your company's assets, liabilities, and equity for a particular period.

- *Statement of Cash Flows*
  It only takes a few minutes to run a report like this. This gives you a quick glance, a summary if you will, when it comes to income and expenses. In it, you'll see your bottom line for a specific period in your overall operations. It can be a week, a month, a quarter, or the year in total.

- *Profit and Loss Statement*
  As its name says, this shows you all transactions classified under general cash flow. This means sales, expenses, and simple transactions. From this statement, you'll see all of the different transactions that have a direct effect not only on your investing and financing cash flow, but your operating funds as well.

- *Comprehensive Financial Statement*
  With the comprehensive financial statements, you get a full year-end report highlighting all activities of the business — from investments to expenses — and assessments or analyses of the company's current financial situation. This is a set of reports prepared by a certified public accountant. With the help of Quickbooks, the accountant can generate these statements much easier, quicker, and with less potential errors than if it were done manually.

6. Tax Management

Tax season is the time most dreaded by all kinds of businesses no matter how large or small they are. Accountants normally have to consolidate multiple reports, receipts, and other documents to ensure that tax returns are prepared properly and filed on time. Quickbooks helps users manage their daily transactions, and consolidates all data come the end of the fiscal year. This means that all they have to do is pull up the data that they need, and the system will automatically start the necessary computations; no more backtracking or double-checking needed. Not only does this allow for the task to be finished quicker, but it also ensures accuracy in the figures.

Chapter 6: The Different Versions of Quickbooks

Quickbooks is one of the first options that will be recommended to anyone who's in the search of simple yet reliable accounting software. And considering how it has been over two decades since the first version was launched, it's quite admirable that Quickbooks continues to dominate the marketplace and resonate with businesses around the world.

What you need to know about Quickbooks is that it currently holds over three quarters of the market share for financial management tools. And throughout its reign as one of the best business platforms, it has accumulated multiple versions, each with its own set of notable features.

If you're a business owner, what version should you consider then? Should you go for the cloud-based one? Should you consider payroll processing capabilities? Below is a handy overview and comparison of the different versions, categorized, to help simplify your search.

Cloud-Based Accounting for Entrepreneurs

Solo entrepreneurs or freelancers will find tremendous value in Quickbooks' version for the self-employed. It's a cloud-based version of the program that's ideal for anyone who professionally contracts services, from neighborhood landscapers to Uber drivers.

The interface is simple and straightforward. There are 6 menu buttons available:

- Home
- Income
- Spending
- Miles

- Taxes
- Accounts (apart from the Feedback function)

At the top right-hand corner, the user will immediately see how much is owed for the next tax period and when this amount is due. Income and spending-related transactions for review are displayed at the center, with transactions for either category color-coded for easier referencing.

Income transactions are recorded as positive (+) while expenses are marked as negative (-). Transaction details are specified, as are payment channels used, to avoid any miscommunication. You'll also find a money tracker comparing how much you've spent versus how much was earned during a particular period.

There are two versions for this Quickbooks release: Self-Employed and Self-Employed Tax Bundle. Both offer access to the same features, namely:

- Bank and credit card accounts linking
- Income and expense tracking
- Transactions categories (Personal or Business)
- Quarterly tax calculation

Now, the tax bundle option offers a couple more features, such as:

- The ability for users to pay their quarterly taxes online (which can save a whole lot of time)
- The ability to easily export deductions marked under Schedule C to TurboTax (which is a tax preparation software developed by the same company)

The self-employed version of Quickbooks is ideal for those who are just starting out with their digital recordkeeping. Out of all its benefits, entrepreneurs will definitely love the ease of usage, and the availability of a mileage tracker. When it comes to the latter, users can log any deductible trips that they take. They can specify the date, the purpose of the trip, and how many miles were driven, and the software will automatically calculate the corresponding deduction.

If there are any drawbacks to this version, it's that it's basic in the features that it offers, making its use limited to smaller-scale businesses. It also doesn't have any capabilities when it comes to creating and filing invoices, and has yet to offer a link to any payment gateway.

Cloud-Based Accounting for Small Businesses

There was a shift in the behavior of consumers back in 2014. As the developers of the software discovered, more customers were starting to favor the online version over the desktop release. And since 2014, the consumer base of the company has grown to exceed a million subscribers. This just shows that small businesses are becoming more and more confident when it comes to utilizing cloud-based accounting software.

For small businesses, Quickbooks has its cloud-based software offering. As with the entrepreneurial version, this one has multiple quick-access buttons as well:

- Home
- Customers
- Vendors
- Employees
- Transactions
- Reports
- Sales Tax
- Apps

On the interface, what you'll see first is a snapshot of the different collectibles and payables due to and from the business.

These are categorized as unbilled, unpaid, and paid; and are color-coded for easy referencing.

The snapshot highlights total amounts, which can be clicked on, after which will display the breakdown of said totals. When it comes to the latter, the details are further categorized by the customer or vendor name, and then subcategorized into different transactions.

For ease of access, users can apply batch actions to the available options, sort, and search. If need be, there are also quick access buttons for sharing and printing. Some of the actions that can be performed on these items include sending reminders, and receiving payments. With such actions, users can better manage their invoices on the platform, and remain on top of things without much effort.

For this version of Quickbooks, there are three packages that you can choose from: Simple Start, Essentials, and Plus. All three packages share similar features, namely:

- Accounts payable and receivable monitoring
- Income and expense management
- Billing and invoicing capabilities
- Unlimited invoice estimations
- Unlimited invoice sending
- Recurring invoice capabilities (for Essentials and Pro only)
- Expense tracking (normally applies to supply and travel costs)
- Financial reporting capabilities
- Access to pre-built report templates (Simple Start has 20, there are 40 for Essentials, and there are 60+ for Pro with the latter including templates for tax and sales reports)

When it comes to the additional features that subscribers can enjoy per package, they are as follows:

1. Simple Start

    - Single user license (the software can be used by only one account)
    - Data import capabilities (Quickbooks desktop to online, Excel to Quickbooks online)
    - Two-user access (two individuals can access the platform under the licensed account)

2. Essentials

    - Features of Simple Start
    - Three user licenses
    - Bill and payment postdating
    - Ability to set specific user permissions

3. Pro

    - Features of Essentials
    - Five user licenses
    - Inventory tracking
    - Purchase order creation
    - Purchase order sending

The great thing about the cloud version is that it's highly connected. This means that users can access it on the go or via mobile apps. Quickbooks can function on Windows, iOS, and Android-powered devices. It also allows for convenient integration with third-party apps like Shopify and PayPal, making it even more convenient to utilize on a daily basis.

If there were any drawbacks to this version, it's that there are still several functionality issues being encountered by users (compared to the desktop version which most of them deem as more complete). For example, the cloud-based software doesn't allow users to run multiple tax IDs. This means that you can only run one company per session.

Desktop Accounting for Small to Medium Businesses

As previously mentioned, there are over a million users who simply love the online version of Quickbooks. But this doesn't mean that the desktop version is inferior. What you have to understand is that both versions offer similar capabilities; they simply differ when it comes to the depth of these features.

A good example will be the user's access to pre-built report templates. It's been mentioned that the Pro online version offers 60+, while the desktop equivalent offers over a hundred of these report templates, plus options that are specific to various industries. But just like the online version, there are several packages under the desktop umbrella. The ones you'll read about here cover 2016 releases.

- Quickbooks for Mac
  This is ideal for smaller-scale businesses. It's compatible with iOS but isn't scalable.

- Quickbooks Pro
  If you have a small business and want to start using accounting software, then this is the version to consider. The great thing about the Pro version is that it can be upgraded to either the Premier or Enterprise versions.

- Quickbooks Premier
  Scalable to the Enterprise version, this package is ideal if your small business has needs that are specific to an industry.

- Quickbooks Enterprise
  Small-to medium-scale businesses will find value in this version. This is because the Enterprise package offers

more flexible business solutions, and a more complex financial management platform.

As users upgrade their packages, they'll gain access to more advanced functionalities. But all of these versions share the same base features, which are as follows:

- Core accounting capabilities (accounts payable and receivable, bank reconciliation, and general ledgering)
- Limited payroll capabilities covering manpower hour tracking, check printing, and deposit slip printing (you can pay for an enhanced payroll upgrade if needed and this will come with tax form filing and payroll tax calculation features)
- Automated billing and invoicing (covers creation, collection, and sending)
- Order tracking, sales and delivery monitoring, and other inventory management components
- Trend tracking and visualization
- KPI assessment capabilities
- Profitability assessment capabilities
- Generation of profit and loss statements
- Balance sheet and other financial reporting capabilities

Here's a more in-depth overview of each desktop package:

1. **Quickbooks for Mac**
   As mentioned, the desktop version of Quickbooks for Mac cannot be upgraded, as this feature is solely available to Windows releases (Pro, Premier, and Enterprise). But this doesn't discount the reliability of the software still. There are several quick access buttons on the left side of the interface, plus an income tracker with color-coded entries for unbilled, unpaid, and paid transactions on the platform.

   When it comes to a small business, there are several financial components that you have to deal with on a daily basis. Quickbooks makes it simple for you to see all of these things via the interface. Apart from payable and receivable totals, there's also a breakdown of your account balance on the dashboard. Here, you'll see everything — from the balance of your checking and savings accounts to any expenses incurred within the period. Think of it as a quick view of your business' accounting balance sheet.

You'll also be better able to monitor your income and expenses via the income and expense trend report, income breakdown, and expense breakdown. The first comes in bar graph form, while the other two are rendered in pie charts. These make it easier for users to assess their spending habits within a certain period of time. Should they find the need to make adjustments, they can immediately determine which areas need to be reevaluated.

With the Mac version, users also gain access to different tracking sheets. It's possible to access data on the company, customer transactions, vendor transactions, employee payroll, bank obligations, reports, and so on.

In line with pricing, there's a one-time fee charged per user license. Usually, a license provides access to a maximum of three unique users.

Depending on what the business needs, potential users can also avail of 24/7 customer support for an additional fee. Phone support plans are available per 90-day contracts.

As per features unique to this version, here they are:

- Income tracker dashboard with unpaid invoice category
- Project accounting capabilities for projects in progress
- Fiscal year budget management and monitoring tools

The thing about Quickbooks for Mac is that data can only be shared with Windows users after it goes through a data conversion process called round tripping. Unless this process is undertaken, an accountant (via accountant view) might not be able to see all data on the platform. Nevertheless, this still remains to be a viable software version alternative, especially since it has been designed to easily integrate with several iOS applications, thereby enabling Apple users to utilize the platform in their native environment.

2. **Quickbooks Pro**

Quickbooks Pro is still simple enough for new businesses to start with. You don't really need to have a wide grasp of accounting to maximize its use, and the best part is that you can easily share any system data with your accountant.

Just like the previous version, users will get a snapshot of their accounts, payables, and receivables on the dashboard. It shares relatively the same features plus add-ons such as:

- Bill tracker for purchase orders, unpaid bills, and the like
- Sales and expense trackers in multiple currencies
- Data import capabilities (Excel, old Quickbooks version, or Quicken to the current platform being used)

A one-time fee applies to the Pro version. Users can also avail of other features like customer support, product upgrades, and data backup services. This version is also available on a "plus package" which simply means that the user will be on an active subscription for the software. The subscription can be renewed annually, and users automatically get updates and upgrades whenever these are released by the developers. As an added bonus, 24/7 customer support and data backup come free with the package.

Should a business want to avail of Quickbooks Pro yet don't have any existing IT infrastructure, they can purchase the software and make use of cloud-hosting services instead. This is a convenient and cost-effective alternative for those who want to reduce their IT costs by a significant margin. With the cloud-hosting service, users can then remotely access the system via a virtual desktop on different devices. This allows for more convenience, greater connectivity, and extended ease of use, making it ideal for people who are always on the go.

The version allows three unique users to simultaneously access the system per license purchased. It can also manage as much as 14,000 list entries across different categories (customers, vendors, employees, company, and the like). The only downside to this version is that it still isn't able to support the automatic downloading of bank transactions (credit card data included). This is a feature that users have to pay for separately on this version, but is available when they use Quickbooks online.

3. **Quickbooks Premier**
   If your business has needs that are specific to an industry, then you'll find value in Quickbooks Premier. It was specifically developed with small business owners in mind, with consideration for industries that are professional, retail, non-profit, contracting, or manufacturing in nature. But unlike other versions, this one comes with a more complex dashboard.

   On the home display, users will see the different primary categories that apply to their business, such as the company, vendors, customers, employees, and bank. Users will then see the different activities housed under these categories. What makes the version unique is that it also presents how these activities are linked to one another, even if they overlap from one category to the next.

Quickbooks Premier shares the same features as the Pro version, but offers these additional components:

- Job estimates and costing
- Forecasting
- Budgeting
- Reports generation by project or client (take note that this version offers over 150 industry-specific templates)

The only drawback here is that users have to shell out a little bit more to enjoy features such as online customer payment processing, and electronic invoicing. Other than that, it's an ideal type of software that can definitely be beneficial to a small or medium-sized business.

In terms of pricing, a one-time payment applies to the purchase of this software, with additional fees for upgrades. In this case, up to five individuals can work on the system at the same time. The plus package setup also applies to this, and vying for the annual subscription means getting phone support and data backups for free. Depending on what a client needs, this version also works with cloud hosting, which is available for an additional fee.

4. **Quickbooks Enterprise**
   Out of all the desktop versions available, Quickbooks Enterprise is the most comprehensive one. Not only does it help you manage the financial aspects of your business, but it also helps with several operational components. Unlike other versions, it comes with applications like Quickbooks Payroll, for example. It's still meant to be used by small-and medium-sized businesses, but on a larger scale. This is why up to 30 user licenses can be purchased per system.

   Think of it as your digital ledger and balance sheet on steroids. Instead of just showing you totals or simple breakdowns of your transactions, it goes the extra mile by categorizing these into varying lapse periods. You gain access to aging lists, which means that transactions are segmented into current ones, 1-month maturity, 2-month maturity, 3-month maturity, and anything in excess of 90 days.

Particularly for businesses with specific needs, having access to a comprehensive platform offers much convenience — but it does come with a sizeable investment. Compared to simpler versions, one license here can amount to three times as much as the former. But considering the benefits, they can easily outweigh the costs.

Users can avail of Quickbooks Enterprise via annual subscription as there's no one-time fee option available for it. The cost also covers phone support, data backups, and software upgrades. If necessary, businesses can opt to make use of cloud-hosting services as well.

There are three packages available when it comes to this particular version of Quickbooks: Silver, Gold, and Platinum. Users will gain access to all features found in the Pro and Premier versions, plus add-ons such as:

- 14 user roles
- Multiple and simultaneous access to the system
- Expanded tracking lists for vendors, customers, employees, and inventories (users can access around 14,500 for the Pro and Premier versions but Enterprise allows access to 100,000 list items)

But there are even more unique features available to users depending on the package that they choose and these are as follows:

- Silver
Provides tools for advanced reporting. These include access to over 150 report templates, auto-fill

capabilities, a help portal, and search functionality for ease of use.

- Gold

Apart from advanced reporting capabilities, this package makes enhanced payroll components available to users. In this case, taxes are automatically calculated, and the system can be used to file these year in and year out.

- Platinum

With this version, users get access to both advanced reporting and enhanced payroll features, plus advanced inventory tools that include FIFO costing and multiple inventory tracking (by location). Advanced pricing tools are also provided — users can monitor quantity discounts as well as any price changes applied to items on the system.

Quickbooks App for Those On The Go

Apart from the different versions and their respective user features, there are a handful of apps available under the Quickbooks umbrella. The purpose of these apps is to improve the functionality of the software. These can be purchased as add-ons to any version:

- Quickbooks POS

This is a cloud-based point-of-sale system that can be accessed on iPads. It makes it easier for businesses to track sales and inventories, and accept credit cards on the fly.

- Quickbooks Payroll

Business owners can automate their payroll disbursement with this feature. It allows them to pay up to 50 employees either by bank deposit or check. This makes generating payroll simpler, as it also calculates taxes, and files year-end tax forms on the company's behalf.

- Quickbooks Payments

With this app, users can send invoices via email, or accept online payments via ACH transfers (electronic bank-to-bank transfer), or credit card.

Chapter 7: The Various Features of Quickbooks

Quickbooks is the type of accounting software that provides its users with access to a comprehensive range of services and features. There are nine primary features that make this a great option for people who are looking into better managing their accounting, namely:

1. **Accounting on the Cloud**
   With Quickbooks, users can choose to go either with the desktop or online versions. Either way, there's always cloud-based access provided. The great thing about this is that businesses have a way by which they can access their records whenever they need to, from wherever they may be, and regardless of what device they have on hand.

   Apart from accessing their account, they can also manage their business on the fly, and make informed decisions quickly. For any business, this kind of mobility results in more seamless operations, and better potential outputs for the business and its employees.

   With cloud access also comes a heightened sense of organization. There really is no excuse anymore as to why records haven't been updated and whatnot. On the plus side, this also eliminates invoices from piling up, getting misplaced, and other potentially costly mishaps.

2. **Ease in Expense Tracking**
   No matter how small a particular transaction may be, jotting it down in your records at the soonest possible time ensures that you don't forget to do it later on. Also, making sure that transactions are noted down in a timely manner reduces the kind of pileup that all paper-pushers simply abhor. With Quickbooks, expense tracking

becomes simpler and more organized as you can access the system anytime, anywhere.

You can record your expenses for monitoring purposes, and make sure that everything's accounted for come tax season. If you want to have a record of the actual receipt, you can also take a picture and save it in digital format within the system. This means that you can finally say goodbye to those folders, boxes, and space-consuming file cabinets.

3. **Simplified and Effective Invoicing**
Now that you've reduced your receipt collection in the office, you can do the same for your invoices. With Quickbooks, you can not only create custom invoices with a few clicks, but are also able to generate sales receipts, estimates, and professional invoices that you can send to your customers, vendors, and partners within minutes.

If necessary, you can keep copies of these within the system, again in digital format, for referencing. The beauty of this feature is that you don't have to waste time managing hard copies. You can also save money as there really is no more need to have invoice pads and the like printed out.

4. **Rapid Reporting**
Manually drawing up accounting reports can be quite a hassle, especially during filing season. Quickbooks makes the task easier by having different kinds of report templates pre-built into the system. All you really have to do is note down your business' transactions on the platform, and when the time comes to generate a report, you simply click a few buttons and it's generated in a few minutes. Simple enough, right?

This makes it easier for users to see how the business is doing and take quick action right then and there. These reports can be drawn up, printed out, emailed, or even customized to fit whatever it is that you need.

5. **Management of Cash Flow**
   For your operations to run seamlessly, you have to keep a close eye on your cash flow. With Quickbooks, this task is easier to accomplish as you can easily input vendor billings into the system. This way, you can monitor which bills have been settled, which ones you've yet to pay, and when the due dates are. If you have regular monthly or annual transactions, you can program these recurring invoices on the system as well.

   As they say, it's a good practice to maximize debt maturities. With a system that monitors due dates, you can make sure that you pay bills only when they're due and not a day earlier (so that you can use the funds for other business needs). This also helps you see to it that you won't miss due dates (which can easily result in penalties, not to mention a loss of trust from your partners).

6. **Multiple Accounts Access**
   Unless you're the working accountant of your business, you need a professional to give you a hand. And unless this professional works with you daily, you need to give him or her access to your records. With a manual system, he or she needs to go over a ton of things before being able to start creating reports. Also, if you've created your own accounting system, he or she must first figure things out.

   Quickbooks is designed to work with accounting standards. This means that anyone will be able to use it, as one system is applied across all versions. There's no need to figure out what goes where or how things have been computed, for example. Also, you can designate users with different permissions (or levels of access) on the system. This means you can share the platform with your accountant, but keep some parts of your operations private if need be. The accountant will also be able to access the system remotely, so working together will surely be a breeze.

7. **Automated Backups**
With the desktop version, you can use a backup feature. Online, the system gets backed up every single day. This means that all changes you make to the system are automatically reflected, including any new tax figures that have been mandated in your area. This also means that all activity on the system is recorded, so backtracking will be easy.

Being able to see updated information when you access the system ensures that you get the right details about your business' financial condition. As a result, you can make quick decisions when you see fit. You can rely on the information presented to be accurate and correct.

8. **Heightened Data Security**
There are many people who still think that the Internet isn't the safest place to have valuable information stored. In most cases, it really isn't. The thing about Quickbooks, even if you decide to work online, is that the developers have made sure that the platform runs on bank-level security. This means that no one except you and your trusted partners will be able to access your business' financial records. Data encryption is applied to all components, ensuring that your data will always be safe from prying eyes.

9. **Access to Unlimited Support**
When it comes to software, tech support should always be available so that all users can get the assistance that they need, when they need it the most. With Quickbooks, standard support is available 17 hours a day, 5 days a week. But users also have the opportunity to avail of 24/7

phone support if necessary. This ensures that they will never get lost on the platform.

Chapter 8: How to Navigate Quickbooks

Quickbooks was designed to be easy to use regardless of your expertise when it comes to accounting software. Here are some simple instructions that will help you navigate Quickbooks so that you can be more confident when it comes to using the program. With this simple guide, hopefully you won't experience setbacks when it comes to locating files, performing functions, and generating reports.

Start by logging in. As soon as you do, you'll be directed to your account dashboard. From here, you'll be able to see all of your business' important financial information. Now, depending on the version that you purchase or subscribe to, there may be certain details present in one interface which varies from the rest. In general, you'll see levels when it comes to your profit and loss.

Instead of a list of transactions, you'll immediately see the net totals for this. Basically, a positive figure corresponds to profit, while a negative balance means that you're on the losing end for the period. These numbers are broken down so that you can see how much income you've generated so far, and how much you've been spending in terms of general expenses.

When it comes to the latter, it's broken down even further into a pie chart so that things are even easier to understand. As your expenses will surely be broken down into categories, these are reflected on the chart so you can easily determine which facet of your business has the most expense, may it be from COGS (cost of goods sold), equipment, legal fees, or any other outflow component.

You'll also see your unpaid invoice balances categorized as overdue (what you currently owe), and how much of what's due you've deposited payments into. There's also a section where you can see how much people (clients, vendors, or other business partners) owe you. Of course, a line graph charting your company's sales levels will be displayed on the dashboard. With this snapshot, you won't have to scurry about to find these essential pieces of information, and will know where your company stands financially right then and there.

There's a toolbar on the upper section of the interface. It comes with a handful of useful buttons, too. By hitting the "Create" button marked by an "X" on the top right-hand corner of the interface, you can generate invoices right then and there. Other functions that correspond to customer, vendor, employee, and other actions can be accessed here as well.

Beside the "Create" button is a magnifying glass icon. Click on it if you want to search for specific files. You can run searches based on file names, dates, and even check numbers. There's also an option to run an advanced search here, which you can use if you have more details on the data you're looking for. The advanced search actually makes file checks quicker as generated results will almost always include the exact file you're interested in accessing.

You'll have other functionalities that can be accessed via the navigation bar on the left side of the screen, some of which are the Dashboard, Banking, Invoicing, Expenses, Employees, and Reports. There's also a "Send Feedback" option there. Click on any of these and you'll be directed to their corresponding landing pages bearing all relevant documents and templates under the category.

If you need to look for something specific and don't know which option it's housed in, simply go back to the top toolbar and click on the gear icon. Do this, and you'll get a menu with options related to your account, available lists, system tools, and even the Quickbooks profile. Should you need to access logs for budgeting, accounts reconciliation, and the like, you'll also find these options via the gear icon.

As you can see, Quickbooks is a program that's quite easy to navigate. Even someone who's new to the platform will have a relatively easy time working with the different available functions. This is why accounting tasks can be completed in a shorter amount of time — not to mention with better ease and accuracy — when they're coursed through Quickbooks.

Chapter 9: How to Create Financial Reports Using Quickbooks

To know where your company stands, you need to look into financial reports like the balance sheet, profit and loss, company snapshot, and so on. With Quickbooks, all these can easily be generated and shared with your accounting partners within operations, during tax season, and/or fiscal year report filing.

There are different kinds of reports that are available on the platform. Some of them are geared toward giving you a better picture of your current operations. Others can be used to highlight income and expenses, or receivables and payables. There are those that are perfect for monitoring stock levels and the like, and you have reports that are meant for taxes and government declaration requirements.

All of these can be accessed with a few clicks, and are generated based on the available information on your account. If you need to customize certain fields, you can certainly do so. Here's a breakdown of the available reports you might like to generate:

- Accounts Receivable Report – What's owed to you
- Customer Balance Summary – Open balances per customer
- Customer Balance Detail – Unpaid invoices per customer
- Collections Report – Overdue invoices per customer
- Statement List – Statements sent per customer
- Receivables Aging Report – Pending collections per period (30, 60, 90, +90 days)
- Receivables Aging Detail – List of pending collections per customer
- Invoice Report – List of invoices per indicated period (date range)
- Accounts Payable Report – What you owe and when they need to be settled
- Inventory Reconciliation Report – Your stock on hand
- Expense Report – Cash outflows and purchases
- Taxable Sales Report – Taxable items in your system

- Sales Tax Liability Report – How much you owe in taxes per agency
- Taxable Sales Detail – List of taxable sold items in your system
- Employee Management Report – Usually includes payroll files
- Balance Sheet – Shows ledger transactions side by side
- Profit and Loss Statement – Shows income versus expenses
- Comprehensive Financial Statement – Inclusive of multiple reports to account for the overall condition of the business for an entire fiscal year

On the platform, you can create any of these reports simply by choosing one from the dropdown menu. You can then choose to customize the fields of the pre-built templates depending on the report requirements you need to fulfill.

Generating reports is quite easy. Here are the processes for two of the most commonly generated report types on the program — the balance sheet and profit and loss statement:

- **How to Generate the Profit and Loss Statement**
  A number of people also refer to the P&L as the income statement. When it comes to tax filing season, this is an essential document that your business simply can't do without. With the profit and loss statement, you should make it a point to review it more than once during the year. This is because it gives you a summary of your company's financial performance for a given period of time. Reviewing it weekly, monthly, or however often you wish can help you make smarter business decisions and alterations moving forward. Here's how to generate a P&L on Quickbooks:
    1. Go to the navigation bar on the left side of your screen and look for the Reports button.

2. When you're in the Reports center, you can click on the recommended tab (doing so will display the list of common reports done on the platform), or choose to click "All Reports."

3. From the latter, choose the "Business Overview" category (report types are categorized for easier navigation), then select "Profit and Loss", then click on "Run" to open the template.

4. You'll see fields that can be edited such as the date range. You also have the option to make other changes to the available template. All you have to do is click on "Customize."

5. Apply the customizations to the template by clicking on the "Run Report" button; otherwise, the alterations won't be reflected on the system.

- **How to Create a Balance Sheet**
  The balance sheet presents ledger transactions: the assets, liabilities, and equity of your company. You can say that it's the snapshot of a business' value. Basically, it starts with the liabilities being subtracted from the assets. The resulting figure is the equity.

  For accountants, the balance sheet gives insight into the business' financial health. For banks, it gives them an idea of whether or not your company is worth investing in or taking a risk on (loan). For business owners, it shows whether or not the business is doing well at any particular moment.

  Similar to your profit and loss statement, the balance sheet is also essential for your accountant. To make it even easier on everyone, do consider working with the more detailed version, the Balance Sheet Detail, which presents balances from the previous month. This makes it easier to make assessments from the past month to the current, as well as make it simpler to generate projections for future months. Here's how to generate a balance sheet on Quickbooks:

1. Go to the navigation bar and click the "Reports" button.

2. Click "All Reports."

3. Select the "Business Overview" category, select "Balance Sheet Detail," and then click "Run."

4. Click "Customize" if needed. You can choose to add the balance field (balances from the previous report) here.

5. Apply your changes by clicking "Run Report."

Chapter 10: How to Perform Basic Accounting Functions in Quickbooks

Accountants have to think about many different functions when they do the number crunching. In Quickbooks, there are different tools that help with these functions, simplifying even some of the most critical tasks. These tools can be found in the Accountant Center that can be accessed via the Accountant menu on the dashboard.

Here are some of the most commonly used features in this section:

- **Delete or Void Transactions in Batches**
  Multiple transactions can be removed at one time, thus making the deletion process simpler and faster.

- **Enter Transactions in Batches**
  Multiple transactions can be copied at one time from one file to another with this tool. Now you won't have to repeat the copy process for every single file.

- **Clear Up Un-deposited Funds Account**
  Accountants can easily link any deposits that have been created manually to the right payment records.

- **Compare the Inventory Valuation and the Balance Sheet**
  This will help the accountant review valuations on both sides to see if they match. It checks both the summary of inventories and inventory account, and displays all transactions side by side for easier assessment.

- **Find Any Incorrectly Paid Liabilities in Relation to Payroll**
  If there are any tax liabilities associated with your company's payroll data that have been settled using a check, this tool will list them all down for easier tracking.

- **Fix Any Incorrectly Recorded Sales Taxes**
  You'll see payments that may be categorized as sales tax payments, but weren't properly recorded. This will help you identify which of these should be, but haven't been recorded via the Pay Sales Tax function. This way, you can make the necessary alterations before tax season.

- **Fix Any Unapplied Customer Payments and Credits**
  The accountant can determine which payments or credits need to be applied to any particular invoice.

- **Fix Any Unapplied Vendor Payments and Credits**
  With this, accountants can quickly determine which bills are open and apply the necessary credits or payments.

- **Merge Vendors**
  The accountant can clean up vendor lists by merging duplicate names whenever he or she sees fit.

- **Reclassify Transactions in Batches**
  Even when you automate your accounting processes, human error may still affect your records. It's a good thing that there are tools that can help you fix these errors, and fast. If you input transactions into the system and tag these under the wrong account, you can find them with the reclassify tool and sort them into their correct account categories.

- **Review List Changes**
  Accountants will be working on multiple lists, from payroll items to those for fixed assets, items, and even charts of accounts. This tool will provide them with a summary of any changes made to these lists.

- **Troubleshoot Inventory**
  Inventory problems can come in different forms. With this tool, the accountant can change the classification or status of certain items depending on any criteria that the business owner has set for these.

- **Troubleshoot Prior Account Balances**

The books of clients and their accountants usually don't match the first time around. It's important that these figures are aligned come review and filing season. With this troubleshooting tool, you'll be able to see where the balances are different. The system will also suggest which entries you might want to correct to match both books.

- **Working Trial Balance**
  Apart from beginning balances and transaction totals, this tool will also include any adjustments and ending balances in the working balance that it will generate for the company's review.

- **Write Off Invoices**
  Surely there are more than a handful of invoices that accountants have to deal with per client or per vendor. In this case, a certain set of invoices can be written off with one action. Quickbooks will also generate a credit memo for whatever has been written off, and attach copies not only to the credit memo itself, but also to the invoice in question. This is so you won't forget about the write-off when you review your files.

Chapter 11: Troubleshooting

As with any other kind of software, there may be times when you'll experience kinks in the system. Although you can't say for sure when these'll manifest and what kind of issue might present itself, it's good to have some knowledge on several of the common issues that normally affect Quickbooks users.

Here are some of them:

1. **Data File Update**
   Updating is important as it ensures that all the information you enter into the system is at its most current. And when it comes to this software, you might encounter problems when you try to update the data file. However, do know that this is an issue that normally occurs when you upgrade your program to a newer version. In most cases, the problem happens because functionalities in the newer version can't accommodate older data files.
   In this case, make it a point to back up your old files first. Also, don't delete the old version until you've successfully migrated all files onto the upgraded system. It will help if you also run file verifications during the migration process.

2. **Data File Rebuilding**
   Particularly with something as serious as financial data, you want to avoid corruption at all costs. But there are times when data rebuilding can pose quite a challenge. Even if you've verified data files to function without issue on a newer version, they still won't, so you have to rebuild it from the old version. The way to go about it is such: Back up your data, verify the file, and then rebuild the file.

   Don't panic if the rebuilding fails. First, make sure that the file can be found on the local machine — more ideally in drive C:\. This means that your file can be on the Quickbooks Q:\ drive as long as it's not located in a shared folder. If it is, the system will think that it's on a different machine and won't read it properly. Do your rebuild on C:\ before you move the file back to Q:\.

3. **Lost Data File Connection**
Losing connection to the file may be one of the most challenging issues to troubleshoot, but it can be done. Even if you're working with the desktop version, having access to a reliable network connection is important, especially during the file updating process. For the online version, you need to have a steady connection to the network because even the shortest glitch can cause problems while you're working.

There's a connection diagnostics tools available on Quickbooks, and you can run it to help you identify potential problems within the system. Also, check your antivirus and firewall settings. There are times when limitations within these programs can be blamed for lost connections.

4. **Failed Installation**
Depending on how often the system fails, or if you simply need to change a few things on your computer, you might find the need to reinstall Quickbooks. What you have to know is that you shouldn't simply go for the traditional uninstall. There's actually what is known as a clean uninstall.

Start by uninstalling the program the traditional way, but go back to your computer's program files. On Windows, these are C:\Program Files\Intuit\Quickbooks(version number) and C:\Windows\Users\Documents And Settings\Program Data\Intuit\Quickbooks(version number). Make sure that you delete both of these after you've backed up your files.

5. **Software Lag**
   System slowdown is an issue not exclusive to software, but it can happen. If you're dealing with lag, it can either be due to hardware issues, or problems with the data file. To remedy this, go to "File" and click on "Utilities" where you can find the "Clean Up Company Data" tool. Run this, and check if the system speeds up. If it doesn't, disable the "Audit Trail" component.

6. **Failure to Locate the Data File**
   Can't find a data file? Check your server machine — the Server Manager should be installed there, and it should be running. If it still fails to work, what you have to do is map the drive and connect to the client server. If you can find the data file then, this means that the Server Manager hasn't been enabled from your end.

7. **Lost Licensing Information**
   Since user licenses for Quickbooks are purchased, you'll have a unique product number with your version. It usually comes with ample documentation as you might need it every now and then for verifications and upgrades. If you misplace it, simply open the program and click on [F2] or [Ctrl]1.

   However, the easiest solution is to write down the validation code the moment you get it (or at least have a duplicate, emergency copy available). If the [F2] or [Ctrl]1 solution doesn't work, you'll have no choice but to register again (during the reinstall process).

8. **Problems with the Printer Link**
   You can create invoices and reports and then print them out. But what if your new printer won't cooperate? Here's what you have to do:

   - Close the program.

- Look for qbprint.qbp on your system.
- Rename it to qbprint.qbp.old.

It should work by the time you restart Quickbooks.

9. **Login Failure**
People lose passwords or forget them; it happens all the time so don't worry. In this case, you can recover any admin access codes by using the "Automated Password Reset" tool.

10. **Failure in File Sharing**
One of the best features of the software is easy data sharing. But if you can't move or copy files, chances are it's because the file was locked. All you have to do is go to the directory monitor or server manager to check if it's indeed locked. To unlock it, close the program, and then click Start or Run. Enter services.msc, look for Quickbooks, and then stop both the server manager and directory monitor. This should allow you to copy or move the file with ease.

If you happen to encounter other hurdles, or issues not discussed here for that matter, check with Quickbooks' phone support.

Chapter 12: Quickbooks Shortcuts

To help make using Quickbooks even easier and quicker, this chapter includes a comprehensive list of keyboard shortcuts for Quickbooks.

Learning a few of these will without a doubt make you more efficient at using the Quickbooks software!

You may use these shortcut keys to access QuickBooks Help Window:

- Function: Display Help in context

Shortcut: F1

- Function: Select next option or topic

Shortcut: TAB

- Function: Select previous option or topic

Shortcut: SHIFT + TAB

These shortcut keys also work for all QuickBooks versions.

You can use the following QuickBooks shortcut keys at various points throughout this small business accounting software program to help with tasks such as displaying information about QuickBooks, opening a new company file, and canceling processes:

- Function: To start QuickBooks without a company file

Shortcut: CTRL + double-click (while opening)

- Function: To suppress the desktop windows (at Open Company window)

Shortcut: ALT (while opening)

- Function: Display information about QuickBooks

Shortcut: F2

- Function: To cancel current process

Shortcut: ESC

- Function: To close active window

Shortcut: ESC or CTRL + F4

- Function: Record (when black border is around OK, Next, or Prev button)

Shortcut: ENTER

- Function: Record (always)

Shortcut: CTRL + ENTER"

If you are looking for shortcut keys for editing dates, characters, and other data in QuickBooks, this list notes some keyboard shortcuts to use:

Modifier Key	Key	Description of shortcut
date field)	[	Same day in previous week (in
date field)	]	Same day in next week (in
Shift	=	Next day (in date field)
Shift number by one	=	Increase check or other form
Ctrl	A	Open account list
date field)	Apostrophe	Same date in next month (in

	Backspace	Delete character to left of insertion point
Ctrl	C	Copy selected characters
Ctrl	D	Delete check, invoice, transaction, item
	Delete	Delete character to right of insertion point
Ctrl	Delete	Delete line from detail area
	Down Arrow	Line below in detail area or on report
Alt	Down Arrow	Date calendar
Ctrl	E	Edit transaction selected in register
	End	End of current field
	Enter	Record (when black border is around ok, save & close, save & new, or record)
Ctrl	Enter	Record (always)
	Escape	Close active window
Ctrl	F	Find transaction
	F1	Open help for active window
	F2	Display product information about your QuickBooks version
Ctrl	G	Go to register of transfer account
	H	Last day of the month

Ctrl transaction	H	History of A/R or A/P
	Home	Beginning of current field
	Hyphen	Previous day (in date field)
	Hyphen	Decrease check or other form number by one
	i	Quickzoom on report
Ctrl	I	Create invoice
Ctrl	Insert	Insert line in detail area

Chapter 13: Frequently Asked Questions

Here are some of the frequently asked questions about Quickbooks' versions and features:

1. **Payments Function**

    - Is there a separate process for bank transfers and credit cards?

        You do not need to repeat the sign-up or set-up process if you want to work with both credit cards and bank transfers. Quickbooks Payments can manage different payment formats within the same account, so you can choose the best channel for your needs.

    - Do I have control over payment options?

        Yes. You can decide on which payment option you wish to extend to your clients. You can add a "Pay Now" button to your invoices and choose to turn on the credit card option, the bank transfer option, or both. You can also change this option per invoice.

    - Are bank transfers free of charge?

        When you apply this payment option, you only pay $0.50 per bank transfer payment; it doesn't matter how much the transfer is.

    - Is the GoPayment app integrated into Quickbooks?

        If you're using the GoPayment app, you can manually download all payments made to your Quickbooks account. In doing this, you can either close an existing sales receipt, or match the payments with any open invoice.

- If I'm using an old version of Quickbooks, how do I update my data?

    If you plan on upgrading your Quickbooks account, your files will automatically be updated when you open them in the new version. Don't worry, your files will be backed up in the old system first just in case you need to access an earlier version later on.

2. **Basic Payroll**

- What do I need to access it?

    You need to be connected to the Internet so that the program can download the most current tax rates and payroll formulas. You need to have an EIN (Employed Identification Number) as well, since this will be reflected in all forms and returns. If you don't have this yet, you can get one via the IRS site.

    If you'll be accessing it as a feature of Quickbooks, your version should be at least Pro or Premier 2011. If you'll be using it as a standalone program, you don't need to have Quickbooks.

- Do I have to use it during the start of the fiscal year?

    No, you can use it mid-year if that's your situation. But you'll have to input past payroll transactions into the system. There is a step-by-step guide available on the website to help you out. If this is your first time paying employees, then there's no need to go through the other steps.

- Does it only work for employees with regular salaries?

    No, it can also help you with payroll for employees that work by the hour.

- Does it handle other payments on top of salaries?

  Yes, you can input commissions, bonuses, and other additional payouts into the system.

- Does it handle payroll deductions?

  Yes, you can incorporate these into the system. Some deductions that the program can manage include sick time, vacation leave, medical coverage, dental insurance, 401(k), cash advances, retirement plans, and so on. You can customize the system to apply specific sets of deductions for each employee as well.

- Can it help me with taxes?

  When you upgrade your system, it automatically downloads the most recent tax and benefits tables as mandated by the government. However, you won't get access to tax forms with Basic Payroll. For this, you need to subscribe to the Enhanced Payroll version. Nevertheless, you can still create reports via this program and work with your accountant when it comes to tax file requirements.

- How do I pay my employees?

  All you have to do is input their regular wage or enter their hours worked and the system will automatically do the computation for you. It will also subtract all deductibles, taxes included. You can then print out the checks or proceed with a direct deposit.

  If you just so happen to have different payment dates for your workers, you can conveniently manage them through Basic Payroll as standard deductibles are programmed into the system when you upgrade. You can shift from weekly to bi-weekly to monthly pay, without having to worry about incorrectly computed taxes and benefits.

Should you decide to go with the direct deposit option, you can make deposits into any US bank account. All Basic Payroll subscriptions come with free access to the direct deposit function, which is installed in the program. If you use Intuit Pay Cards, you can also deposit the money here.

The great thing about the direct deposit option is that you can add or remove employee information at any time. You're also not limited to just this option when releasing pay. You can pay some employees via check, while others via deposit.

It's important though that you send all deposit transactions by 5 PM Pacific Time at least 2 working days before salaries are due. This ensures that your employees get their money at the right time. If needed, you can also deposit salaries into 2 accounts (maximum) per employee. Salary summaries can easily be viewed online so there's no need to print out pay stubs.

- Is it safe to use?

  Yes. All data is protected by the same kind of encryption used by banks, so your information will be safe especially on payday.

- Can I share payroll information?

  Yes, you can. You can easily email the files and reports to your accountant directly from Basic Payroll.

3. Enhanced Payroll

- What do I need in order to access it?

  It's important that you have a stable connection to the Internet because the system needs to download all current tax rates and payroll tables. The program will also ask you for an EIN (Employed Identification Number), and this will be present in the forms and returns that you generate via Enhanced Payroll. You can easily get an EIN from the IRS website.

Your version of Quickbooks should be at least Pro or Premier 2011 if you will be using it as part of the system. However, you can also purchase Enhanced Payroll as a standalone program. In this case, you won't need a subscription to Quickbooks.

- Do I have to use it during the start of the fiscal year?

    No, you can use it mid-year or anytime, actually. You will just have to input past payroll transactions into the system if applicable.

- Does it handle other payments on top of salaries?

    Yes, all you have to do is input other additional payouts like bonuses and commissions into the system.

- Does it handle payroll deductions?

    Yes. Just like additional payouts, you can also program deductibles into the system. Everything from vacation leave, to sick time, to medical and dental coverage can be managed by Enhanced Payroll. You can also include deductibles such as 401(k) and other pension-related figures, plus cash advances if there are any. Deductible computations can be programmed to be unique per employee.

- Can it help me with taxes?

    Yes, but note that you need to be connected to the Internet so that the program can automatically download the most recent tax and benefits tables as mandated by the government. Unlike the basic program, you get access to tax forms with the enhanced version. You can work on these ones from the system: W-2, W-3, 940/Schedule A, 941/Schedule B, 944/945a, 943/943a, 1099-MISC, and 1096.

Should there be any other form that you need but can't find on the system, don't worry. Enhanced Payroll will provide you with a State Tax Summary report that you and your accountant can use. You also have the option to file your taxes and make payments online, through the platform.

- How do I pay my employees?

    The process is the same as with the basic version: Just key in your staff's regular wage or enter their hours worked and the system will automatically calculate the paychecks for you, subtracting all deductibles, taxes included.

    You can also program the payment dates (i.e. weekly, bi-weekly, monthly) for your employees if they have varying salary schedules. Again, don't worry because the program will do the math for you.

    What's more, if you're not physically around come payday, you can still pay your workers via the Quickbooks mobile app.

4. **Quickbooks Online**

    - What should I do to start?

        Go in for a startup interview on the site. This will help you determine the best version to try or buy.

    - How much is it?

        According to the Quickbooks website, the following plans are priced as such:

Simple Start - $10 per month
Essentials - $17 per month
Plus - $30 per month

There is also an option for freelancers which is priced at $5 per month.

Meanwhile, the add-ons such as Enhanced Payroll and Full Service Payroll are priced at $19 and $49 per month — applicable to two (2) employees — respectively.

- What do I get when I subscribe?

    You get full access to your chosen version's features, integration with various apps (PayPal, Shopify, TSheets, American Express, Square, and more), and automatic upgrades that are free of charge. Data storage and product and chat support services are free as well. It's possible to upgrade the program's features at an added monthly cost.

- What other features come with the program?

    It comes with several pre-built reports (estimates, invoices, expenses, payments, taxes, etc.). Depending on your plan, you can have shared access among multiple users for better collaboration.

    All plans come with the Receipt Capture feature, which is great way for you to manage and organize receipts without the clutter. Just snap a photo of the receipt using your phone camera, and the digital copy will be automatically synced with the program.

- Can I add more features?

    Yes. You can easily upgrade the software with more features when you see fit. Note that additional charges may apply to these features.

- Is there a demo or user tutorial?

    Yes. Please visit the website to access these. You can also register for Quickbooks' live webinars, which are held weekly. These one-hour sessions cover not just Quickbooks navigation for beginners, but also provide tips and how-to's on accounting, bookkeeping, and managing your business' finances, from sales to overhead expenses.

- Do I need to know accounting to be able to use Quickbooks?

    Quickbooks can be used by anyone, even the non-accounting literate. Simple instructions and 24/7 chat support are available so it won't be any problem at all for anyone to get started.

- Can I import data from a non-Intuit program?

    Yes, but data files need to be converted first. To do this, users should contact Intuit's support team.

- How do I download the online program?

    There is no need to download the program as it can simply be accessed online via the Quickbooks site.

- What are the system requirements?

    - High-speed, stable Internet connection
    - Desktop Browsers: IE 10, Safari 6.1, Firefox, Chrome
    - Mobile Browsers: Chrome (Android), Safari (iOS 7)
    - Mobile Devices: Android phones and tablets, iPhone, iPad

    However, do note that on mobile devices, access to certain features may be limited.

- It is only compatible with Windows?

    There is a specific version designed for Mac systems. On Linux, the program can only act as a database server for storing data files.

- Do I need to constantly be connected to the Internet?

    The online version needs a constant and stable connection to the Internet.

- Does it come with data backup services?

    Data is backed up daily and the server maintains a duplicate copy of your data files. Records are updated up to a certain period though, so this means that you can't restore any data or settings that lie beyond this point.

- Is it safe to use online? What is the level of data privacy?

    Yes, it's safe to use online. The platform uses bank-standard transmission technology. All data are also encrypted.

- Can I download my data?

    Yes, you can download a copy of all data for personal storage.

5. **Online Trial**

    - Where do I access it?

        Simply visit the website and click the "Try It Free" button to begin.

    - What happens to my data when I start a subscription?

Your data automatically gets migrated to your subscription, provided that you get one that's a higher version compared to your chosen trial version; if not, you have to manually reenter all information. If you don't avail of a subscription, your data will remain in read-only mode after the trial expires. It will then be deleted after 90 days.

6. Quickbooks Desktop

- Where can I find the desktop version?

  You can access it via the website.

- What are the system requirements?

  - When working on Windows, these are the compatible versions: 8.1 7 SP1, and Windows 10
  - You can work with either the 2016, 2012 R2, or 2008 R2 SP1 servers.
  - 2.4 GHz capacity processor
  - At least 4 GB of RAM but 8 GB would be better
  - At least 2.5 GB of disk space as you need ample storage for data files
  - Unless you'll be using the Intuit server, you need a 4x DVD-ROM drive.
  - At least 1 Mbps Internet speed is essential for you to access online features and payroll add-ons.
  - Product ID or registration code
  - Optimization for 1280 x 1024 or a higher screen resolution
  - Supports one workstation monitor, plus extended monitors (maximum of 2)
  - Optimization for DPI settings in default
  - Browser: IE 11

- Can it be integrated with other programs?

- The program can be integrated with these MS Office versions: Office 365, 2016, 2013, or 2012.
- Data can be transferred from these Intuit programs to your current Quickbooks version: MS Office 365, MS Excel 2016, 2013, 2010, Quickbooks 2004 to 2017 (only 2016 for Mac), and Quicken 2015 to 2017.
- To integrate reports, invoices, and other forms, you need to use: MS Office 365, Microsoft Outlook 2010 to 2016, Outlook.com, Yahoo Mail, Gmail, or SMTP-supporting e-mail clients

7. Desktop to Online Switch

- How do I switch from desktop to the online version?

  Instructions can be found at the program's Import Resource Center.

- Is there a demo for the online version?

  Yes, you can access it via the website.

- Can I try the online demo before I switch?

  Yes, you can try it out first.

- Do both versions offer the same features?

  Many features may differ between the online and desktop versions, as the former is designed for users who need to access their data files and work while on the go.

There may be other inquiries you'll require clarifications for. In this case, you can always contact the company's support line. Depending on the Quickbooks version you're subscribed to, you may have access to the 24/7 chat support. If not, there's always their phone support service that's available 5 days a week.

Conclusion

Thanks again for taking the time to read this book!

You should now have a good understanding of Quickbooks, and be ready to get started with the powerful program!

If you enjoyed this book, please take the time to leave me a review on Amazon. I appreciate your honest feedback, and it really helps me to continue producing high quality books.

Made in the USA
Columbia, SC
29 March 2019